Old SOUTH AYRSHIRE VILLA

by
Hugh Maxwell

A farmer shepherds his sheep along the main road leading from Colmonell to Ballantrae. On the left are the entrance gates to Knockdolian House. The large parish of Colmonell, which stretches from the coast to the border with Galloway, comprises mostly of hills and weather-beaten moorland and is very sparsely populated. Its seclusion made it a favourite haunt of Covenanters and the area had several martyrs to this cause, one of whom, Matthew McIlwraith, is buried in Colmonell churchyard. His tombstone states that in 1685 he was shot dead by a party of dragoons under the command of 'Bloody' Claverhouse. The body then lay in the woods of Dangart Glen for several days until it was wrapped in a grey plaid and carried to the churchyard by two young women, who also dug the grave. Other stones in the churchyard include those of John Lusk, a farmer at Pinmore Mains, whose son Andrew became Lord Mayor of London, and of William McAdam of Ballochmorrie, who died in 1836, the son of the celebrated road builder John Loudon McAdam.

Text © Hugh Maxwell, 2003.
First published in the United Kingdom, 2003,
by Stenlake Publishing,
Telephone / Fax: 01290 551122

ISBN 1 84033 240 9

FURTHER READING

The books listed below were used by the author during his research. None
of them are available from Stenlake Publishing. Those interested in finding
out more are advised to contact their local bookshop or reference library.

Rob Close, *Ayrshire & Arran – An Illustrated Architectural Guide*, 1992.
Rev. James A. Guthrie, *A Corner of Carrick*.
Rev. R. Lawson, *Places of Interest about Girvan*, 1892.
Rev. R. Lawson, *Views of Carrick*, 1894.
James Edward Shaw, *Ayrshire 1745–1950: A Social and Industrial History of
    the County*, 1953.
John Strawhorn, *Ayrshire – The Story of a County*, 1975.

ACKNOWLEDGEMENTS

The author wishes to thank the staff of the reference departments at the
Dick Institute, Kilmarnock, and the Carnegie Library, Ayr, and also the
many people of South Ayrshire, in particular Gordon Clark, who
contributed information towards this book. The publishers wish to thank
the following for contributing photographs to this book: Gordon Clark
for pages 2, 8, 9, 11–15, 17, 18, 22, 24, 25, 28–30, 35, 36, 38, 42–44, 46 and 48;
and Alex McGowan for the front cover, inside front cover and pages 1, 4–
7, 10, 19–21, 23, 26, 27, 31–34, 37, 39–41, 45 and 47.

Tom Aitken the Postmaster standing with his wife in the doorway of the
little post office at Daljarrock. Tom would often be seen cycling all the
way up to 'The Barr' (as the village of Barr was known) to deliver and
collect the mail there. Translated from the Gaelic *dail dharach*, Daljarrock
means the 'dale' or 'field of the oaks'. This cottage has since been
demolished.

INTRODUCTION

Until 1186, South Ayrshire – or the district of Carrick as it was known – was part of the Kingdom of Galloway, but in that year it became permanently separated when Duncan, son of Gilbert of Galloway, inherited the land and became the first Earl of Carrick.

The second Earl of Carrick had no male heir, but left a daughter who became Countess of Carrick. She married the Lord of Annandale and on 11 June 1274 gave birth to Robert the Bruce at Turnberry. When Robert was eighteen the earldom fell to him and he retained the title until 1313. Crowned King of Scots in 1306, Bruce was subsequently forced into exile by the English, but in 1307 he relaunched his bid for control of Scotland by landing at Maidens in 1307. One of the first actions of his army in the campaign which eventually culminated with the Battle of Bannockburn was the successful storming of Turnberry Castle and the routing of the English garrison stationed there.

At that time the landscape was covered with forest and animals such as wild boar, deer and wolves roamed the largely uninhabited area. What local people there were made their living from the forest or the sea and over the decades most of the original woodland disappeared.

Throughout the sixteenth and seventeenth centuries the district was continually embroiled in bitter feuding among the landowning families and there were many infamous incidents involving open fighting, bloodshed and murder. The most powerful family were the Kennedys who often fought with the Campbells of Loudoun and the Craufords of Kerse. The Kennedys also had inter-clan conflicts, particularly between the branches of Cassillis and Bargany. Due to this unrest many castles and keeps were built in the region – the map of South Ayrshire surveyed by Timothy Pont prior to 1608 shows the existence of a staggering 160 and today there are still twenty-nine in existence.

As these feuds ran their course the local landlords turned their attention to improving their lands and estates. Mansions were constructed and land reforms were implemented to provide work for their tenants. The last period of unrest was during the seventeenth century when the ministers of South Ayrshire were staunch supporters of the Covenanting cause. The tombstones of many Covenanters can be found within the churchyards at Barr, Straiton, Dailly and Colmonell, and dotted across the countryside are numerous memorials and monuments to those persecuted in those dark years.

By the turn of the eighteenth century great improvements had taken place in agriculture and small commercial fishing fleets were also based at Dunure, Maidens, Girvan and Ballantrae. Markets were being held regularly at Straiton, Dailly, Barr and Colmonell. On the Water of Girvan and its tributaries there were fifteen corn and waulk mills, with an equal number on the River Stinchar and as many again dotted along the shoreline. By 1837 early potatoes were also being extensively harvested due to the favourable soil and weather conditions which meant that saleable crops could be produced much earlier than elsewhere in Scotland. Ayrshire potatoes became much in demand, with thousands of tons being shipped overseas to America and to other parts of the British Isles, and the harvests continued to be successful until the early 1920s when, as a result of continual planting in the same fields year after year, yields and quality began to decline.

There is evidence of coal mining in the Girvan Valley from as long ago as 1415, but by the late 1700s an extensive industry had developed in the area surrounding Dailly, at pits such as Killochan, Maxwell, Drummochreen, Dalzellowlie and Kilgrammie. Production increased dramatically in the first half of the nineteenth century as a result of the Industrial Revolution, but unfortunately this coal was mostly used only locally due to the excessive cost of carrying it to the coast for export and the lack of a suitable harbour at the principal town of Girvan.

The late eighteenth and early nineteenth century also saw the expansion of the handloom weaving industry. Due to a huge influx into the area of migrant workers from Ireland and the Highlands, and the building of large cotton mills in Glasgow and Paisley, there was a tremendous demand for weavers to ply the shuttle, spin the yarn and produce webs of cotton for the manufacturers. As a result many villages and hamlets grew and expanded. The weavers were initially well paid, earning between thirty and forty shillings for only a four-day week, but disaster struck in the 1860s when cotton shipments to Britain ceased due to the outbreak of the American Civil War. Left unable to earn a living, many weavers and their families were forced into poverty and deprivation. Later, the development of the powerloom and the machine production of lace and other textiles finished off their industry and many people emigrated or moved away to live and work within the large lace mills at Kilmarnock, Paisley and Glasgow. Throughout South Ayrshire homes were simply abandoned and by the end of the 1800s the populations of many communities had fallen sharply.

Becoming prevalent from the eighteenth century onwards, smuggling – principally of tea, tobacco, salt and brandy – also contributed to the development and prosperity of the communities along and just inland from the coastline. However, increased activity by Revenue officers and the Admiralty, combined with the reduction of duty on excisable goods, eventually saw this way of life vanish.

In 1869 the railway was extended to Girvan, reaching Stranraer six years later, and this brought many holidaymakers in from the industrial centres. In 1906 the Glasgow and South Western Railway also constructed a new coastal line to Girvan from Ayr via Maidens, Turnberry and Dunure, and this also attracted visitors. Tremendous prosperity and growth resulted from the annual influx of holidaymakers and until the 1950s the villages along the coast flourished as popular seaside resorts during the summer months.

After the Second World War, agriculture proved to be much less profitable due to increasing mechanisation and competition from overseas and there followed much diversification with large areas of land being planted with commercial forest. With the development of larger, more cost-efficient vessels, fishing also steadily declined. Resorts on the coast also suffered greatly as a result of the boom in foreign package tours, although the popularity of the area among coach and motor day-trippers has undiminished.

In recent years there has been a slow migration of people back to the South Ayrshire villages, attracted by the charm and tranquillity they have retained, and although the area has changed considerably over the centuries, it remains a landscape unrivalled and renowned for its historical heritage and natural beauty.

'Ballantrae' derives from the Gaelic *Baile-an-Traigh* which means 'the village upon or above the shore'. The ancient name of the parish was Kirkcudbright Innertig, but in 1617 an Act of Parliament ordered the moving of the parish church, which was formerly at the mouth of the River Tig near Knockdolian, to Ballantrae and hence the name of the town gradually took the name of the parish. This scene from around 1905 looks westwards along Main Street with several of the horse-drawn brakes of the popular Girvan and Ballantrae Coaching Tour parked in the street. On the right are the trees in front of the United Free Church, adjacent to the small lane that leads up to the public hall, manse and bowling green.

Ballantrae's church dates from 1819 and the clock tower and grey spire were added in 1891. Inside the church are bronze memorials to David MacGibbon of the Victorian double act MacGibbon and Ross, a postman who died in a blizzard at the top of Glenapp, and a gamekeeper who died in another blizzard on Beneraird. Just to the left of the church are the trees surrounding the graveyard, which contains the Kennedy monument and tomb. Dating from 1601, this was built in memory of Gilbert Kennedy who was the last of the great Ardstinchar lairds. He was the sixteenth Baron of Bargany, but at the age of twenty-five was killed at Maybole that year during a feudal conflict with his cousin, the Earl of Cassillis. The only other remaining monument to this once great family are the remains of Ardstinchar Castle, which stand on a rocky height overlooking the main road just to the south-east of the village.

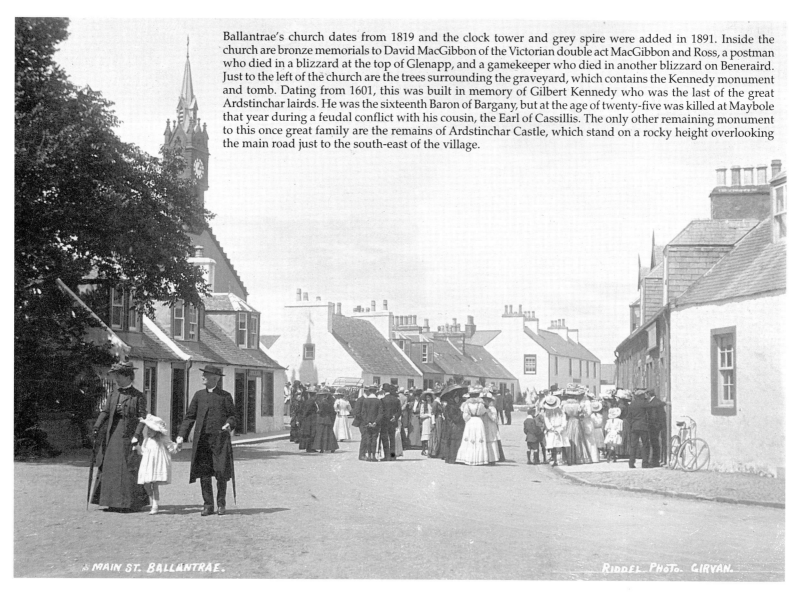

MAIN ST. BALLANTRAE. RIDDEL PHOTO. GIRVAN.

Foreland, Ballantrae.

Although it has since expanded to become part of Ballantrae proper, Foreland was once considered a separate community and comprised several rows of single-storey thatched fishermen's cottages which were built by the Girvan Building Society in the early nineteenth century. The cottages stood adjacent to the small tidal harbour, pier and quay, which were constructed in 1847, at great expense, from Arran freestone. To help exploit the potential for fishing, it was necessary to excavate the basin from solid rock at a cost of £6,000. Most of the money was raised by the Board of Fisheries who made a grant of two-thirds of the total sum, with the heritors and the fishermen subscribing the remaining third. It later became a calling point for the Stranraer to Glasgow steamers *Nimrod* and *Loch Ryan*, but the harbour is now only used by small fishing craft and pleasure boats. In the foreground of this view stands the semaphore signal station, with the road on the right leading back to Main Street where the coastguard station was located.

The hulk of the Danish schooner, *Richard*, which was driven ashore during a strong gale in October 1926, on the coast just north of Ballantrae. The dark bulk of Bennane Head dominates the background. Penetrating deep into this rocky headland is a cave which was associated with the legend of a lost piper and which was also used by smugglers to conceal and store their contraband. Its narrow entrance shows signs of once being fortified and it was perhaps also used as a prison. At the top of the hill are the ruins of the old Craignaw Inn which was famous as being the headquarters of the smugglers. More sinisterly, the cave was supposedly the lair of Sawney Bean and his savage gang of cannibals in the sixteenth century. It was reputed that this family of cannibals lived there for around

THE SHORE AND BENNANE, BALLANTRAE.

twenty-five years, butchering as many as a thousand people who had mysteriously disappeared from the surrounding area during that time. When the family and their crimes were discovered they were captured and taken to Edinburgh for execution. The men were bled to death by having their hands and feet chopped off, while all the women and children were burnt alive in three large fires. In 1832 the brothers Chalmers visited this part of the country and wrote in their *Gazetteer of Scotland* that the dwellers were 'till within the last twenty or thirty years, almost as wild and rude as the remote Highlanders of Ross-shire, though no doubt a great deal wealthier. And what the natural circumstances of the district gave rise to was greatly influenced, at one period, by the lawless state into which much of the population was thrown by smuggling. It is not yet more than forty years since the immense bands of people who, in this district, attend funerals, would fall out on the road to the parish town, where the churchyard is situated and, without regard to the sober character of their duty, set down the corpse and fight out their quarrel with fists, sticks and such other rustic weapons as they happened to be possessed of, till, in the end, one party had to quit the field discomfited, leaving the other to finish the business of the funeral. Brandy from the French luggars that were perpetually hovering on the coast was the grand inspiration in these unseemly brawls.'

The roadside village of Colmonell – pronounced 'Com-mon-ell' by the locals – is located on the rising ground in the glen of the River Stinchar, four miles north-east of Ballantrae. The name is derived from the church, which in the twelfth and thirteenth centuries was called Kirk-Colmonell in memory of the patron saint Colmonella who died in 611. The present parish church was built in 1772, with further alterations being made in the nineteenth century by Robert Lorimar. In this view a number of horse-drawn coaches of the Ballantrae Coaching Tour have stopped in Main Street to allow their passengers some refreshments at the Queen's Hotel. With several large wooden chests on the pavement it would appear that many tourists were planning on staying in the village for their holidays. Most of Colmonell's original houses were built on the north side of the street, but in 1936 council houses were built on the south side. The village has a long reputation as one of the most attractive villages in South Ayrshire and in the past its praises were frequently sung by local bards – 'A beauty, in a beauteous dell,/Serenely fair sits Colmonell'.

Colmonell is approached via the Bush Bridge, before the road enters what was known locally as the 'Kirk Wynd' and then turns sharply to head along Main Street. In past times the only other access to the place was from the ford on the river where the current stone bridge (built in 1867) now stands, and from where the imposing ruins of Craigneil Castle can be seen perched across the valley on a knoll of limestone rock. Formerly belonging to the powerful Cassillis family, it was built in the thirteenth century by Neil, Earl of Carrick. Three stories high, with walls over 6 feet thick, it is a massive tower which commands an excellent view of the entire Stinchar valley. According to tradition, the castle was reputedly one of the places used by Robert the Bruce and his army. This view taken around 1917 shows Main Street, with the small grocery and provisions store on the left displaying postcards of local views that were always popular with holidaymakers.

The Street, Colmonell

By the 1950s the population of the village was only 280, but nonetheless it still supported two churches, two hotels (the Boar's Head Inn and the Queen's Hotel) and six shops. In earlier times four fairs and markets were also held at the village. This photograph shows the view eastwards along Main Street, with a horse and cart standing outside the post office on the left. Further along the street are the ornamental railings and gates outside the entrance to Kirkhill Castle which is behind the houses on the left. Next along is the public hall and further on is the smithy, the United Free Church manse, the village school and the United Free Church (built in 1898).

Today, a small village of around 160 inhabitants, Pinwherry was established at the confluence of the rivers Duisk and Stinchar and the junction of the main Girvan–Newton Stewart and Ballantrae–Colmonell roads. Later, there was a little station (closed in 1956) on the Glasgow and South Western railway line, in addition to the current sub-post office, school, community hall, general store and forty houses of varying sizes. The village took its name from Pinwherry Hill, while not far to the south are the ivy-clad ruins of Pinwherry Castle. This dates from around the close of the sixteenth century and was abandoned sometime before 1800. On the left of this view is the village's old toll-house, with the schoolhouse in the background. Near the village is an unusual little monument commemorating the memory of John Snell, one of Scotland's greatest educational benefactors, who was born nearby at Almont. The inscription reads: 'Near this spot in 1629 was born John Snell. Son of Andrew Snell, smith in Almont. Scholar, Soldier, Lawyer, he rose by diligence and prudence to high office in the State, being seal-bearer to King Charles II. He died at Oxford in 1679. To his memory this monument was by public subscription erected in 1915.' In 1643 he studied at Glasgow College under the guidance of James Dalrymple, who later became first Viscount Stair, before becoming a Seal-bearer to the Chancellorship, Secretary to the Duke of Monmouth and the Commissioner for all the duke's estates in Scotland. He made a large fortune and endowed bursaries at the colleges of Oxford and Glasgow.

Daljarrock Post Office stood where the roads from Newton Stewart and Girvan joined and it was a popular resting point for coaches on the Ballantrae Coaching Tour. Daljarrock comprises of nothing more than one or two rustic cottages clustered around the entrance gates of Daljarrock House near the foot of Bargain Hill. This house was the home of Miss Margaret Kennedy whom Robert Burns met in the house of her uncle, Gavin Hamilton of Mauchline. In her honour, Burns composed the song 'Young Peggy Blooms' – 'Young Peggy blooms our bonniest lass,/Her blush is like the morning,/The rosy dawn the springing grass/With pearly gems adorning'.

On the condition that he would actually live there, Captain Euan Wallace, MP, inherited from his uncle 30,000 acres of land to the north-west of Barrhill. Wallace commissioned James Miller, a Glasgow architect, to design a huge house based on the Cotswold-style and work commenced in 1915. It ceased in 1923 with the interior of Kildonan House still largely incomplete, but it had already become the largest, grandest and most expensive mansion ever built in Ayrshire. It had sixty-five rooms, indoor tennis courts and a theatre. Despite having to offer 15,000 acres of his estates in Ayrshire for sale in 1930 due to a shortage of capital, Captain Wallace managed to keep living in the house until his death in 1941. It then became a convent boarding school managed by the Sisters of St Joseph of Cluny until 1976, when it closed down. The house then remained empty for several years. In the early 1980s plans were put forward to turn the house and surrounding policies into a luxury holiday development with purpose built chalets, but this fell through and Kildonan House was converted into a luxury hotel by new owners in 1988. This photograph shows the stable block with its arched gateway and buttressed clock-tower cupola that was also designed by James Miller.

A view of Barrhill, looking west over the old bridge, built in 1811, which spans the Cross Water. In the distance the road can be seen winding its way out of the village towards the Arnsheen Church which is partially hidden by the trees in the background. In the 1950s there were two general merchants, a grocer and baker, a butcher, a small draper and stationer, two confectioners and even a small tearoom and café to cater for visitors. At this time the village had around eighty houses, some of which were council built. There was also a small bank, a hotel, a post office and a local surgery. A notable trade that was once carried on here was the hand processing of fleece to what was called 'wauked roll' and the manufacture of mohair and angora bed covers and scarves, which were produced at the waulk mill where ten people were employed. As can be seen in this photograph there was little in the way of street lighting and it was only in later years that electric light from two Diesel plants were used to provide this. These were run by two local joiners, one of whom supplied one side of the street, while the other took care of the opposite side.

Crosswater, Barrhill.

As can be seen here, the Cross Water, which flows off the surrounding hills and moorland, neatly divides the village of Barrhill into two separate parts before it flows into the River Duisk. Prior to the railway station on the Ayr to Stranraer line being built just to the south of the village, Barrhill was a primitive place with less than one hundred inhabitants. The economy was entirely based on agricultural, with several important markets being held throughout the summer season. Located a considerable distance from the nearest town, the village was also a posting establishment for changing horses on the main route from Girvan to Newton Stewart.

According to the Rev. R. Lawson, in 1892 Lendalfoot consisted of only about six cottages which were clustered around a small school, and in former times the houses had been grouped around a wayside inn. The hamlet later became an attractive holiday resort and by the 1950s as many as twenty-eight holiday bungalows had been built. At one time there was also a thriving fishing industry, remembered in the name of the Carleton Fishery, the group of cottages located just to the south of the village. Lendalfoot is situated in the shadow of Carleton Hill and just out of picture on the left, but clearly visible to motorists travelling south along the main road, are the ruins of Carleton Castle. Perched precariously on the edge of a ridge overlooking the Bay of Lendal, the castle was the ancestral home of the Cathcarts of Carleton, a powerful and influential family within Ayrshire and one associated with a gruesome tale. The castle was once the home of Sir John Cathcart who had a propensity for acquiring wives and their wealth. After marrying such a lady, as soon as the titles for her estate were clear 'fause Sir John' would simply escort her to a rocky outcrop called 'Gamesloup', some two miles south of Lendalfoot, and throw the unfortunate woman over the cliff. Seven or eight brides had met this terrible fate before the next to be treated in this fashion, May Collean, turned the tables on the murderer and pushed him off the cliff. Supposedly, she then inherited all the wealth and titles he had acquired through his misdeeds.

Located just to the south of Lendalfoot is the cluster of cottages, dating from around 1832, known as the Carleton Fishery. Over the years many vessels sought shelter in the Bay of Lendal, only to meet their doom on the rugged reef offshore where there are several hazardous rowes or points, two of which are called the 'Lendal Rowes'. One particular incident is commemorated in a little tombstone, surrounded by a low dyke and railing near the roadside, which bears the following inscription: 'Erected to the memory of Archibald Hamilton and crew, natives of King's Cross, Arran, who were drowned near this place, September 11, 1711.' A small verse is also carved into the stone: 'Ye passengers whoe'er ye are / As ye pass on this way / Disturb ye not this small respect / That's paid to sailors' clay.' Since 1711 the inhabitants of the district have preserved the stone, although near the end of the nineteenth century a ferocious storm washed away a portion of the earth to the right of it, uncovering the skeletons of the drowned fishermen.

Pinmore began as a cluster of houses which were established around the small rural station on the Glasgow and South Western Railway line to Stranraer which was constructed in 1877. The station was used mainly for transporting livestock and for the carriage of timber and other goods. This photograph shows the station, platform, signal tower and stationmaster's house which stood adjacent to the main road and which, after the station closed in September 1965, was converted into a private house. Nearby there was also a smithy, schoolhouse and post office. Just to the north of Pinmore is the Dinvin Motte, one of the finest prehistoric forts in Ayrshire, and just below this ancient earthwork is the equally impressive 496 metre long railway tunnel on the Girvan to Stranraer line. Another feat of railway engineering in the vicinity is the Kinclaer Viaduct (later known as the Pinmore Viaduct), a stone structure of eleven arches with a maximum height of eighty feet. At one time an infectious diseases hospital was sited at Dinvin for the treatment of locals suffering from smallpox.

The conservation village of Barr derives its name from the Celtic 'Bar', meaning a summit or height, and this is a direct reference to the wild and high moorland district of the Stinchar Valley. Barr officially became a parish in 1653, being formed from the outlying areas of the parishes of both Girvan and Dailly, and it quickly grew to become one of the largest in Ayrshire with the fewest number of inhabitants and the greatest number of sheep! One of the original documents relating to the parish bears the signature of Oliver Cromwell. This photograph was taken from the Gregg Bridge and looks north-west across to the village with the rushing Water of Gregg in the foreground and the Kelton Hill dominating the background. On the left is the graveyard and adjacent to this is the two-storey row of houses containing the King's Arms Hotel. Overlooking the village is the house, Kelton Villa.

A large crowd gathered for the opening ceremony of the Carnegie Morton Library on 4 April 1913. Designed by John Arthur and distinctive with its timber gables and attractive red tiles, the village institute, as it is now known, is still at the centre of the village's activities. Another notable building in Barr is the church, which was built in 1878 by Allan Stevenson. An earlier church was the old chapel of Kirkdandie, the ruins of which overlook the Stinchar River near the village. This was the scene of the celebrated fair of Kirkdandie, which took place annually on the last Saturday of May. Held on the green knoll beside the ruined chapel, this market was the only one held locally and many people travelled from quite far to attend. Booths and stands were erected to provide entertainment and to sell and trade goods that were brought on horseback by merchants and pedlars from England and all over Scotland. With as many as forty tents being erected and pipes and fiddlers playing their tunes, these lines from a local ballad describe the scene: 'Some did the thieving trade pursue,/While ithers cam to sell their woo;/And many cam to weet their mou',/And gang wi' lasses hame, man'.

Known by locals not as Barr but as 'The Barr', this photograph dating from around the 1940s shows the view looking down the village's Hill Street towards Main Street. Within the village a small one-storey cottage is known by locals as the Jam Factory in memory of the Rev. John Barr, who organised a job creation scheme in 1918 which involved all the local housewives cooking jam to raise money for the families of those lost in the Great War. The garden and grounds of the cottage later became a successful market garden and nursery. The main road from the village to Girvan crosses over the old Stinchar Bridge (built in 1787) before turning sharply and climbing in a series of sharp twists and turns known locally as 'The Screws'. According to the *New Statistical Account* of the 1840s the population here was at that time only 230, with the inhabitants chiefly employed as weavers, shoemakers, blacksmiths, tailors, masons and farm workers. There were then four inns within the village.

A steam traction engine travelling southwards along Dailly's Main Street. The village derives its name from the Gaelic *dealge*, meaning 'thorns'. In this view the parish church, which dates from 1766, is visible in the background, while on the right is one of the narrow lanes leading to the Back Road. Coal mining was carried out in the vicinity for many years and in the graveyard behind the church stands a monument to the memory of John Brown, a collier 'who was enclosed in Kilgrammie coal pit, by a portion of it having fallen in, October 8, 1835, and was taken out alive, and in full possession of his mental faculties, but in a very exhausted state, October 31, having been twenty-three days in utter seclusion from the world, and without a particle of food. He lived for three days after, having quietly expired on the evening of November 3, aged 66 years.' Deep coal mining continued in the district until the late 1960s.

This unique photograph, taken on the hill behind the school in Dailly, shows smoke issuing from what was known locally as 'The Burning Pit'. At Drummochreen Colliery, about one mile from Dailly, miscalculations in extracting coal and propping the pit workings resulted in the pillars collapsing in 1848. Week after week, the workings went into collapse, the damage travelling uphill and affecting all the seams in its course until finally, on 6 December 1849, the entire workings came crashing down, shaking the ground violently as if an earthquake had occurred. The next day the workings caught fire and the flames soon reached the top of the pit, a distance of some 200 feet, and the pithead was suddenly set ablaze. The fire burned deep within the ground and spread westwards above Wallacetown and eastwards beyond Craigside, resulting in the whole brow of the hill between these two points becoming red hot. Attempts were made to extinguish the fire by flooding, but these had no effect and the area smouldered for many years before the fire gradually diminished, with the only evidence of its existence being the dead vegetation, plumes of steam and the constant discharge of noxious gases and smoke from cracks in the ground.

Workers from the Bargany Estate near Dailly, photographed clearing the channel of the mill lade that served the old mill located just off Dailly's Main Street. Water was taken from the River Girvan to power the mill and it flowed via a small dam dyke off the river itself and two sluices to turn the large breast paddle waterwheel. The mill building had three storeys and an attic which contained four pairs of millstones. One pair was used for shelling oats and also for smutting wheat, one pair for oatmeal, one pair for cattle provender, and the final pair for grinding flour. In addition to being used for corn grinding, the mill was subsequently let to Messrs Adam Wilson and Sons in 1880 and was also used as a sawmill to produce timber products from wood felled on the estate. The last miller was Mr William S. Fettes who retired in 1939 when the mill closed. Seven years later it was demolished and the rubble from the building was used to fill in the lade. The mill's site was later taken by a public park.

Bargany Estate is situated to the south-west of Dailly. Its mansion house was built in 1681 by John Hamilton, second Lord Bargany, using stone from the ruins of Bargany Castle, a former Kennedy stronghold which formerly stood on the site. Nothing now remains of the old castle and in 1980 an application to have the mansion demolished was refused. The house was later extensively renovated to its former condition. Two of Scotland's most famous Victorian poets, Hew Ainslie, the estate baker's son, and Hamilton Paul, the coal grieve's son, were both born within the same small cottage on the estate. Today the beautiful woodland gardens are open to the public throughout the summer season.

Turnberry Hotel was built in 1904 by James Millar for the Glasgow and South Western Railway Company. It was officially opened in 1906 and was connected by a covered way to the station of the Dunure and Maidens Light Railway which was completed that year. Occupying a commanding position above the golf links, the hotel was built in the Georgian style at a cost of £60,000. The total area occupied by the links, which were first built by the Marquis of Ailsa near the end of the nineteenth century, is 180 acres. The historical associations of the locality are represented in the romantic names of the greens, such as Weary Neuk, Bruce's Castle, Ailsa Craig and Turnberry Lights. The hotel remains one of the most popular and famous hotels in Scotland for golfing and the golf club hosted the open championship in 1977, 1986 and 1994.

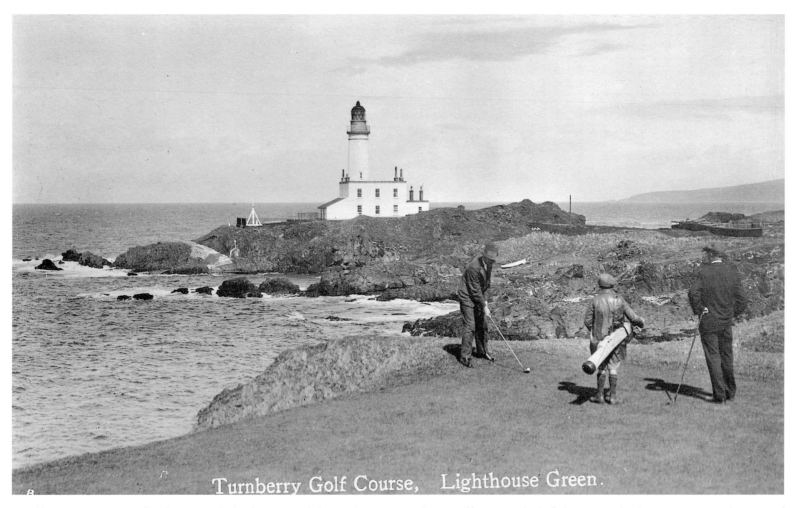

Turnberry Golf Course, Lighthouse Green.

A golfer prepares to tee off a shot towards the famous Lighthouse Green at Turnberry golf course. The lighthouse was built in 1873 next to the ruins of Turnberry Castle. Once the seat of the Earls of Carrick, the castle is probably the oldest building in the district and was the birthplace of Robert the Bruce. In the spring of 1307 Lord Henry Percy's garrison of English soldiers were wiped out within Turnberry village and the castle was seized before Bruce embarked on his perilous journey to ultimately gain independence for Scotland. The lighthouse was built within the courtyard of the old castle and the ditch that once defended it on the landward side can still be seen. Visitors can still put their fingers into the groove that was formed by its portcullis.

SEAVIEW, MAIDENS

Once known as the 'Marquis Village' after the Marquis of Ailsa, Maidens was originally little more than a row of fisherman's cottages and fish-curing sheds along the shore. However, it still managed to support a church, a post office (pictured here), several small shops, a convalescent home, a smithy and a corn mill. From the early 1900s it became popular with holidaymakers and many new houses and holiday homes were built in the vicinity. It was also a very busy fishing port and in the 1950s the local villagers constructed a new harbour pier and breakwater from the rubble left from the RAF buildings at Turnberry which had been abandoned after the Second World War.

Known by locals today as 'The Maidens' this photograph shows the sprawling nature of the village that is clustered around the Maidenhead Bay. Just inland from the village is Douglaston where Douglas Graham (1738–1811) was born and just to the south-east was his Shanter Farm. Like many farmers along the coast, Douglas kept a small boat moored at Maidens for the purposes of fishing, but supposedly he also used it for smuggling. The name of this boat, which was discretely painted on the stern, was the 'Tam O' Shanter' and this proved to be the inspiration for Burns's masterpiece. The letters 'BA. 46' on the hull of the 'La Veronica' in the foreground denote that it was registered in Ballantrae.

The pier and harbour at Maidens date from the eighteenth century. Just south of the harbour there is an ancient monument on top of one of the hillocks, visible on the right, which is believed to commemorate either the death of a great hero or the achievement of a great victory. According to the *Statistical Account* of 1791–99, it is stated that these hillocks are composed of a substance resembling coal ashes. They have existed from time immemorial and were accidentally discovered to contain the ashes, which were used for drainage on surrounding land. 'Although about 1000 cartloads have been taken there remain in the two hillocks, at a moderate computation, above 3000 loads more.' No-one knows where the ashes came from in such quantity, but it has been suggested that they were perhaps the scene of some form of pagan worship as several relics of warfare such as a spear have been unearthed in the area and there are traces of a Druid's circle nearby.

MAIDENS RAILWAY STATION.

The local station on the Dunure and Maidens Light Railway, which was operated by the Glasgow and South Western Railway, stood just to the east of Maidens. The Dunure and Maidens Light Railway left the main line at the Alloway junction, serving the village before later rejoining the main line at Girvan. Locals knew it as the 'Maidens Line', but passenger services were withdrawn in December 1930 with the station being closed and the line completely closing to goods traffic in 1955.

A view looking north-east over Kirkoswald. On the left, in the background, can be seen the Free Church, built in 1777 from a design by Robert Adam, who was also responsible for Culzean Castle, and erected by the Earl of Cassillis. Also visible on the right is the school, with the flagpole, and the large white schoolmaster's house, while further to the right, just out of picture, is the Richmond Hall which was erected in 1924 on land donated by the Marquess of Ailsa. Kirkoswald was once a centre for the contraband trade and Burns himself often witnessed 'scenes of swaggering riot and roaring dissipation' during his brief stay there. Tradition recounts how on one occasion a farmer's wife in the district made porridge with brandy instead of water, and only discovered her mistake when there was an unaccountable demand for more! A skirmish between smugglers and excisemen was fought near the village which became known as the 'Battle of Howshean Moor'. This took place on 27 January 1777 as the smugglers, disguised and armed, mounted a rescue mission to take repossession of goods previously captured by the officers of the excise. Blood was spilt with several men being injured, and a horse was killed, but the smugglers succeeded in their mission.

Kirkton Jean's smithy at Kirkoswald. Adjacent to this can be seen the ruins of the church that was erected early in the thirteenth century by Duncan, Earl of Carrick, and dedicated to St Oswald, the last of the English heptarchic kings slain in 642 at Oswastre. It was in this old chapel in 1776 that Robert Burns worshipped under the Rev. Matthew Biggar, while attending Hugh Rodger's school in the village. Within the graveyard there are many notable tombstones, quaintly sculpted and inscribed with curious epitaphs. There are stones in memory of the Browns, the maternal relatives of Burns, and also to that of Douglas Graham of Shanter, Hugh Rodger, the schoolmaster, and John Davidson, 'Souter Johnny'. Jean Kennedy was the inspiration for Kirkton Jean, the innkeeper's wife in Tam O' Shanter and before it became a smithy the building was indeed an inn. Sadly, it has since been demolished.

Main Street, Kirkoswald
Showing Souter Johnnie's house on right.

In 1775 Robert Burns spent the summer attending Hugh Rodger's school at Kirkoswald and the many characters that he encountered there were the inspiration for *Tam O' Shanter*. In this photograph Souter Johnnie's house with its thatched roof is on the right. The cottage was built in 1785 by John Davidson, the village cobbler, and Burns became acquainted with him at nearby Glenfoot, near the farm of Shanter, where he was lodging. After the death of Davidson in 1808, the cottage was divided into two separate dwellings. It was preserved by a local committee around 1920, before being acquired by the National Trust of Scotland which runs it as a public museum. In the garden at the back of the cottage, carved in stone in 1802 by self-taught sculptor James Thom, are the figures immortalised by Burns in his work. They were exhibited and displayed in many towns throughout Britain before being acquired for the cottage in 1924.

Looking along Kirkoswald's Main Street where the schoolhouse of Hugh Rodger, Burns's teacher, was located. A hotel now stands on the site of the school, but a plaque commemorates its literary importance as Burns reputedly composed one of his first poems there. In Kirkoswald there is also the old font in which Robert the Bruce was supposedly christened. According to the *Statistical Account of Scotland* (published 1791–1799), the parish register dated 1610 to 1620 recorded various flagrant violations of the Sabbath: 'It was, in frequent instances, proved before the session, that persons were guilty of fishing and selling their fish openly in Maybole market; that others winnowed their corn, and gave no reason for so doing, but that the wind was favourable; that others openly washed and dryed their cloaths; and that others were guilty of tuellying, as it is called, or fighting to the effusion of blood, in the churchyard, in the time of divine service. So frequent at that period was the vice of drunkenness, even on the Sabbath, that we find the session enacting, that no inn-keeper should sell on that day more than two pints of ale to a company of three persons. It further appears, from the same register, that the vice of adultery was also very frequent. However, it would seem that the morals of the people began to improve after the year 1630.'

King Street, Crosshill.

The village of Crosshill is a comparatively modern place as the owner of the land only issued feus for the building of cottages sometime around the early 1800s. At this time handloom weaving was the main employer and houses were in great demand by many Irishmen who were attracted to Ayrshire by the work and good wages. Of the 1,000 inhabitants at that time, around 800 were Irish by birth or extraction. This view looks north along King Street as passengers board the bus from Maybole for the bumpy ride into nearby Dailly and then to Girvan.

The view looking eastwards along Straiton's Main Street, with the McCandlish Hall standing on the right. The village's distinctive rows of single storey cottages were built by Thomas, Earl of Cassillis, in the 1760s. The war memorial can be seen at the far end of the street, next to the gates of Traboyack Manse which dates from 1795. In the background, on top of the 1160 foot Craigengower Hill, is a distinctive granite obelisk which was erected in 1856 to commemorate the life of Lieutenant-Colonel James Hunter Blair of Blairquhan, who was in the Scots Fusilier Guards and died at the Battle of Inkermann during the Crimean War. He was also at one time the county MP.

The McCandlish Hall was opened on 22 November 1912 and became a much-used social centre for Straiton and the surrounding area. Its wooden floor was renowned as the best dance floor for miles around and many people would travel by bus from as far as Maybole, Girvan and Dalmellington to attend the regular weekend dances and enjoy the live music once held there. Today, the McCandlish Hall remains largely unchanged and is still at the centre of community activities.

In this view the road sweeps northwards out of the village towards the Water of Girvan. On the right is the junction for the Dalmellington Road, while on the left are the steps leading up to the McCandlish Hall. Just visible through the trees on the left can be seen the tower of the parish church which was erected in 1758, incorporating part of the original kirk and a well-preserved old Kennedy of Blairquhan tomb which dates back to around 1510. The church has two distinct portions, the first being the old aisle with its Gothic window and outside staircase which once formed part of the Roman Catholic Church that stood on the site prior to the Reformation and which dates back to around 1350. The second is the whitewashed modern building that was erected later. The church, which seats 280 people, was restored in 1901 by John Kinross and at this time the tower with its memorial bell was also added. Within the graveyard is a monument to the Covenanter Thomas McHaffie who was shot nearby.

In early documents the village's name was variously spelled as Strattun, Stratton, Strattoun and Strattin and it is no doubt of Celtic derivation from the Gaelic 'strath' and 'don', signifying the 'deep valley'. This is precisely descriptive of the site occupied by the church and village, which stand between two hills on the upper part of the Water of Girvan. This is the view looking north-east along the Dalmellington Road. Half a mile along this road is the wooded Lambdoughty Glen and the aptly named Rossetti's Linn that is over thirty feet in height. It is named after the celebrated poet and artist Dante Gabriel Rossetti (1828–82) who once leapt over the water, while contemplating suicide there.

Deriving its name from St Michael, Kirkmichael was revived around 1790 as a centre for handloom weaving and by the 1830s the manufacture of cotton was the staple trade of the place. The large Glasgow manufacturers appointed agents in the area to distribute the cotton to the handloomers who were then responsible for producing the woven fabric. By that time the village had a healthy population of 560 inhabitants. Located at the east end of Kirkmichael, Kirkport (pictured here) is the area where the road to Patna turns awkwardly to the left around the parish church at the far end, which was built in 1787. The churchyard contains a tombstone which dates from 1506 and also a martyr's monument, erected to honour the memory of the Covenanter Gilbert McAdam who was shot near the village by the Laird of Culzean. In the street can be seen many of the old handloom weavers' cottages which were built during the eighteenth and nineteenth centuries. Just out of picture on the right is the Portcheck Bridge, spanning the Dyrock Burn, which was built in 1775.

In 1923 Kirkmichael House became a convalescent home for miners (which it remained until 1956), although earlier owners had also used it for charitable causes. On 8 June 1908 the *Ayrshire Post* reported that a 'Grand Fête' was held at the house: 'Under ideal weather conditions, the grand fête organised by the Ladies' War Work Committee in aid of their funds, took place in the beautiful grounds of Kirkmichael House, which were kindly lent for the occasion by Mr and Mrs D. McCowan. The grounds were crowded, it being estimated that there was over eight hundred people present. A splendid programme had been arranged by the committee and several bands were in attendance. There were also entertainments, games, sideshows, rowing on the loch in front of the house, fortune telling and many other attractions, which combined to bring pleasure to the many visitors. Delightful open-air concerts were also held and during the evening the well-known 'Aerolite' troupe gave their popular entertainment to crowded audiences. Throughout the day sports were held with over one hundred competitors for the various events such as egg and spoon race, 100 yards men's race and 100 yards women's race. . . . The five-a-side football competition also attracted great attention, there being thirteen teams entered. After good sport the winners proved to be the Dunaskin Engineers with Dailly Thistle a creditable second. The grand total realised by the day's effort amounted to £172.'

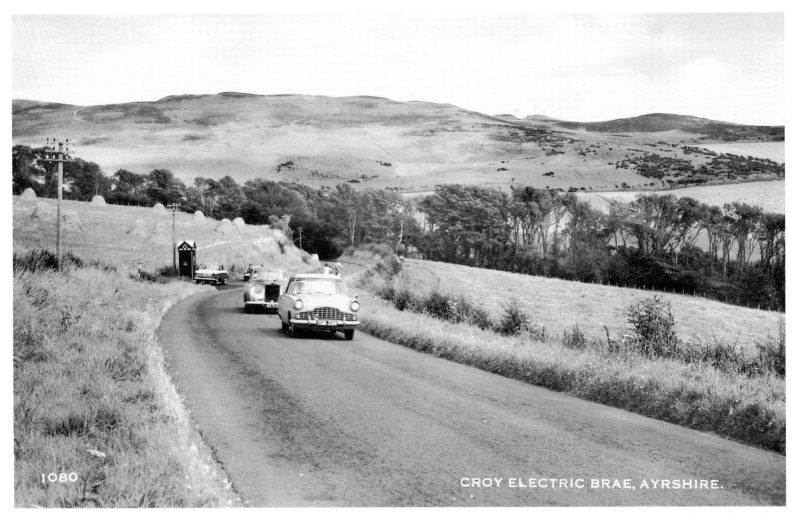

CROY ELECTRIC BRAE, AYRSHIRE.

Bounded to the north by the cliffs of Dunure and to the south by the hills surrounding Culzean, the famous electric brae at Croy, with a gradient of 1 in 86, presents a startling optical illusion to the motorist. The road here has the strange appearance of going up when in fact it is physically going down, and vice versa. This was thought to have been caused by natural electricity or magnetism within the earth and therefore it was named the 'Electric Brae'. Today a granite boulder has been erected at this spot to explain that the brae is actually a natural phenomenon.

The small square harbour at Dunure, reminiscent of those common on the east coast of Scotland, was dug out of solid rock and was much improved in 1811 at a cost of £50,000 for the export of coal overseas. In 1819 leases were advertised here as Dunure was 'a most advantageous fishing station and a place where various trades may be carried on, and a considerable intercourse by shipping may be established; it is believed to posses many recommendations'. This photograph shows the distinctive row of traditional fishermen's cottages on the south side of the harbour, while the small fishing fleet can be seen moored in the harbour itself. Visible on the higher ground, overlooking the old part of the village, are many of the more modern houses that were built, while just out of picture on the right are the now badly eroded remains of the beacon tower at the end of the short pier.

Discharging Herring at Dunure.

Discharging the herring at Dunure was a frequent activity that always drew the attention of onlookers, both locals and tourists. A sizeable fleet operated from the harbour, but trade never developed as anticipated and with the use of larger vessels which could sail much further and catch more it was ultimately lost to the larger harbours on the coast. The Dunure and Maidens Light Railway served the village from 1907 and drew in many holidaymakers, although passenger services only lasted until 1930 with the line closing completely in 1955. Situated nine miles south of Ayr, the village has retained much of its original character, despite the harbour now being frequented more by pleasure craft and the village by day trippers from nearby towns.

Minishant derives its name from the Gaelic *muine seant* which means the 'sacred thicket'. The hamlet was created when the blanket-weaving trade was established here in the late 1700s and two woollen mills were purposefully built by the Limond family, one driven by waterpower and the other by steam, to manufacture blankets, tweeds and travelling rugs. The houses were built predominantly on the west side of the main road. Today the general appearance of the hamlet has changed considerably with the building of more houses. There is now no local industry as the mills closed around 1950.

On the extreme left is Peru Cottage which was painted yellow and named after its owner Peter Tweedily, who built it after returning from South America where he worked as an engineer. The larger two-storey houses were known as Woodlea, the Barracks and the Brick House and also just visible on the right, as the road sweeps out of the hamlet, are the row of thatched cottages housing the blacksmith's, the joiner's shop and the post office. Mrs Margaret Limond was the Postmistress for many years; living to the age of ninety-five, she was renowned as the oldest postmistress in Britain. Just opposite these cottages on the left side of the main road was the location of the water-powered waulk mill, which manufactured everything from wool including blankets, tweeds, flannels and plaidings. The steam-powered mill was located on the crest of the Knowe and a small bogey line was also constructed to winch the coal up to the furnace from the roadside.

Hogg's Corner Minishant

In 1798 the main highway from Ayr to Maybole was constructed with toll-houses at Carcluie and at Mossend at the junction of the Kirkmichael Road. This photograph shows the latter which became known locally as 'Hogg's Corner' after the Hogg family who were its occupants for many years. The toll-house was built against a steep hillside and because of its low roof it was once said that it was possible to step from the field behind directly onto the thatch roof. All evidence of the building has disappeared.

There was once an ancient ford at Dalrymple, but a stone bridge over the River Doon was erected in 1849 – at a cost of £456 3s 2d – to carry the road northwards from Girvan to Edinburgh through Main Street, pictured here. Just south of Dalrymple are the Cassillis Downans, five beautiful little green hills, made famous by Robert Burns in the first stanza of his poem 'Halloween' as the place where the fairies dance – 'Upon that night, when fairies light/On Cassilis Downans dance,/Or owre the lays, in splendid blaze,/On sprightly coursers prance'. From the top of the highest hill, which is about 500 feet in height, the turrets of Cassilis House, one of the oldest baronial residences in South Ayrshire, can be seen among the woods on the banks of the River Doon. It was said that the house was originally intended to have occupied an elevated site at the top of one of the hills, but the fairies were so much opposed to this that they demolished at night what had been built during the day, moving the stones and other materials to the spot where the castle stands today. The owner eventually became convinced of the folly of contending with his supernatural opponents and at length gave up the contest!